Valentine's Stories

20 real cases of passionate love

Phillips Tahuer
Ediciones Afrodita

Contents:

Introduction

Introdución

The Limits of Passionate Love

Love is one of the most universal and powerful forces that has inspired humanity. Love is expected to be a source of support, understanding, and mutual growth, a union based on respect, trust, and shared passion. In its ideal form, love drives us to be better, to face challenges together, and to build a future full of hope and happiness.

However, history shows that love does not always conform to these ideals. Sometimes, emotions and passions transcend conventional boundaries, leading couples to experiences that defy common expectations and reveal both the greatness and complexity of the human heart. These extraordinary loves can be a source of inspiration and creativity, but also of conflict and tragedy.

In this book, we explore a collection of real cases of outstanding loves that have left an indelible mark on history. From the tumultuous relationship of Frida Kahlo and Diego Rivera, where the intensity of their bond fueled unparalleled artistic output but also generated deep conflicts, to the union of Cleopatra and Mark Antony, whose romance not only marked a political era but also led to the collapse of great civilizations.

These stories show us that love can be a transformative force that drives people to reach unsuspected heights, defying social norms and facing adversity. However, they also show how excessive love can lead to destruction, loss, and suffering, revealing the fine line between inspiring passion and destructive obsession.

As we delve into these stories, I invite you to reflect on the multifaceted nature of love. What drives us to love with such intensity? How do we handle the emotions that overwhelm us? And, above all, what lessons can we learn from those who have loved in extraordinary ways, both in their successes and failures?

This journey through historical and legendary love not only celebrates the beauty and strength of love but also acknowledges its challenges and contradictions. Because, ultimately, it is this complexity that makes love a deeply human and eternally fascinating experience.

Phillips Tahuer

Here is a list of 20 cases of passionate love in history, which go beyond the ordinary and reflect the intensity and complexity of relationships. Each one has its positive points, as well as its negative sides.

1. Cleopatra and Mark Antony: The romance that shook the Roman Empire

The relationship between Cleopatra and Mark Antony is one of the great romances of ancient history, a story of love, power, and tragedy that has captivated generations. This intense relationship not only affected the two lovers but also had profound political implications and changed the course of the history of the ancient world. Their romance transcended not only because of the drama of its ending but because of the mix of ambition and passion that characterized their bond, marking the end of the Roman Republic and the rise of the Empire.

Cleopatra VII was born in 69 BC, as a member of the Ptolemaic dynasty, the Greek family that had ruled Egypt since the time of Alexander the Great. She was an intelligent, charismatic, and ambitious woman, known for speaking multiple languages and for her ability to manipulate politics to her advantage. When Cleopatra ascended to the throne of Egypt, the country was facing internal tensions and increasing pressure from Rome, which was the dominant power in the Mediterranean.

Cleopatra is remembered not only for her beauty but for her political astuteness. She knew that Egypt's survival depended on maintaining good relations with Rome and used her charisma and skill to negotiate with some of the most powerful men of the time. Before meeting Mark Antony, she had allied with Julius Caesar, with whom she had a son, Caesarion.

For his part, Mark Antony was a highly renowned Roman general and one of Julius Caesar's closest allies. After Caesar's assassination in 44 BC, Mark Antony allied himself with Octavian (later known as the Emperor Augustus) and Lepidus to form the Second Triumvirate and divide control of Rome between them. Antony was assigned to the eastern provinces of the empire, where his fate would intersect with that of Cleopatra.

Unlike his cold and calculating rival Octavian, Mark Antony was a passionate man, with a penchant for hedonism and grand displays of power. His charisma and bravery as a general won him the loyalty of his troops, but his lack of discipline and tendency to be carried away by his emotions also brought him trouble.

The first meeting between Cleopatra and Mark Antony took place in 41 BC when Mark Antony summoned Cleopatra to explain his loyalty to Rome following Caesar's death. However, Cleopatra came to this meeting not as a submissive sovereign, but as a majestic figure. She made a grand entrance, wrapped in luxury and splendor, and Antony was immediately captivated.

The two shared a deep connection, not only emotional but also political. Cleopatra, seeing in Antony the possibility of maintaining Egypt's independence, forged a strategic alliance with him. But what began as a political arrangement soon transformed into a passionate romance. Cleopatra and Mark Antony became lovers and lived a relationship marked by opulence, luxury, and excess.

Their love blossomed for years, and Mark Antony, who had already been married to Octavia, Octavian's sister, began to distance himself from Rome and spend more time in Egypt. His relationship with Cleopatra became public, and together they had three children: Alexander Helios, Cleopatra Selene, and Ptolemy Philadelphus.

Cleopatra and Mark Antony's relationship was not only a romantic union but also had enormous political implications. Antony granted Cleopatra and her children Roman territories, which was seen by many in Rome as a betrayal. His connection with the Egyptian queen and his rejection of Octavia provoked the anger of Octavian, who used it as an excuse to discredit Antony before the Roman Senate.

In 32 BC, Octavian declared war on Cleopatra, a conflict that also involved Mark Antony. At the famous Battle of Actium in 31 BC, the combined forces of Antony and Cleopatra were defeated by Octavian's fleet. Following the defeat, Antony and Cleopatra fled to Alexandria, where they faced the reality of their defeat and the collapse of their dreams of power.

The end of the story of Cleopatra and Mark Antony is one of the most famous tragedies in history. After their defeat at Actium, both desperately tried to find a way out. Antony, falsely believing that Cleopatra was dead, committed suicide by throwing himself on his sword. When Cleopatra discovered what had happened, she also decided to end her life, according to legend, by letting herself be bitten by a poisonous snake, probably an asp.

With her death, Egypt came under the control of Rome, and Caesarion, Cleopatra's son of Julius Caesar was executed. Thus, the Ptolemaic dynasty came to an end, and Octavian became the first emperor of Rome, marking the beginning of the Roman Empire.

The relationship between Cleopatra and Mark Antony has transcended time because it encapsulates the intersection of politics, power, and love in ancient history. Their romance, which sparked a war and marked the end of an era, has inspired writers, playwrights, and filmmakers for centuries, featuring in plays such as Shakespeare's "Antony and Cleopatra" and iconic films such as "Cleopatra" (1963), starring Elizabeth Taylor and Richard Burton.

The silver lining to their relationship is that, despite the forces around them, Antony and Cleopatra share an authentic and passionate connection. Both, particularly Cleopatra, were charismatic figures who defied the conventions of their time. Cleopatra remains a fascinating figure for her ability to wield power and maintain Egypt's independence for so many years, while using her relationship with Antony to strengthen her political position.

The story of their love also represents the desire of two people to defy fate and the rules of politics to be together, which resonates as a narrative of rebellion against societal norms and expectations of power.

The downside, however, is evident in the tragic consequences of their relationship. Their affair sparked the collapse of Antony's power and the destruction of Cleopatra's kingdom. Mark Antony's decisions, many of which were motivated by his love for Cleopatra, led to a showdown with Octavian, which resulted in the downfall of not only Antony but also Cleopatra and the independence of Egypt. Their relationship, though intense and passionate, isolated them from the real world and made them vulnerable to the political interests of Rome.

Furthermore, their story is a reminder of the dangers of being carried away by personal passions to the detriment of political responsibilities. Antony, by abandoning Rome and placing his loyalty in Cleopatra, lost the favor of his people and his allies. At the same time, Cleopatra, though an intelligent and shrewd queen, underestimated the power of Rome and the extent of Octavian's political pragmatism.

2. Napoleon Bonaparte and Joséphine de Beauharnais: The Love That Shaped an Empire

The relationship between Napoleon Bonaparte and Joséphine de Beauharnais is one of the most famous in history, not only because of the magnitude of the characters involved, but because of the intensity of their love and the complicated dynamics that defined their marriage. This romance was marked by power, passion, politics, and, finally, tragedy. Although it ended in divorce, their relationship has transcended time as a reflection of the complex interplay between personal ambitions and romantic passions in the context of an Empire.

Napoleon Bonaparte was born in Corsica in 1769, and from an early age, he showed immense talent for military strategy. Throughout the French Revolution, he rose rapidly through the ranks of the French army, establishing himself as one of the most brilliant generals of his time. His leadership during the Italian campaigns brought him fame, and he soon became the dominant figure in France, eventually assuming the title of Emperor of the French in 1804.

Napoleon was an ambitious man, determined to expand his empire and establish a legacy to rival history's greatest emperors. However, despite his toughness and determination on the battlefield, he had a more vulnerable side when it came to his personal life, and this aspect was evident in his relationship with Joséphine.

Joséphine de Beauharnais, born in 1763 on the island of Martinique as Marie-Josèphe-Rose Tascher de La

Pagerie, came from an aristocratic family, but one of limited means. She was sent to France to marry Viscount Alexandre de Beauharnais, with whom she had two children, Eugène and Hortense. Her first marriage was turbulent and ended tragically when Alexander was guillotined during the Reign of Terror in 1794. Joséphine, imprisoned during that period, survived and, upon her release, established herself as a leading figure in Parisian society.

Despite the hardships she faced, Joséphine was known for her charm, elegance, and ability to navigate the social complexities of post-revolution France. It was through these connections that she met Napoleon Bonaparte.

They first met in 1795, shortly after she was released from prison. Although six years his senior and a widow with two children, Joséphine's beauty and charisma immediately captivated the young general, who fell deeply in love with her. To Napoleon, Joséphine represented a sophisticated and desirable figure who brought him closer to the French high society that he, as a Corsican and a military man, had not yet fully conquered.

At first, however, the feeling was not mutual. Joséphine, who at first saw Napoleon as just another fling, did not reciprocate Napoleon's fervor with the same intensity. Still, Napoleon courted her passionately, and eventually, on March 9, 1796, the two were married in a civil ceremony, just two days before Napoleon left to command the French army in Italy.

During the early stages of their marriage, Napoleon showered Joséphine with love letters that reflected the intensity of his devotion. While Napoleon was on campaign, he would write to her passionately, expressing his deep desire to see her again. These letters, many of which have survived, show a vulnerable Napoleon, dominated by his emotions toward Joséphine.

The relationship was far from perfect, however. Despite Napoleon's passionate love, Joséphine had multiple infidelities while her husband was on campaign. When Napoleon learned of her betrayals, his unconditional love for her began to mix with resentment and jealousy. Although the general attempted to forgive her, this knowledge deeply affected their relationship.

For his part, Napoleon also began to have his affairs. As his power increased, he surrounded himself with admirers and lovers, although he never stopped loving Joséphine. Their relationship became an emotional battleground, where loyalty and passion constantly clashed with mistrust and deceit.

Despite the tensions in their marriage, Napoleon crowned Joséphine as Empress of the French on December 2, 1804, during his coronation as emperor. This ceremony was a symbol of his public commitment to her, and Joséphine played an important role as France's most important female figure.
Sin embargo, el matrimonio comenzó a deteriorarse debido a la presión que enfrentaban. Napoleón, obsesionado con el legado y la expansión de su imperio, deseaba desesperadamente tener un heredero varón. Joséphine, ya en sus cuarenta y habiendo

tenido problemas para concebir después de sus dos primeros hijos, no pudo darle el heredero que tanto anhelaba.

Ultimately, the lack of a son forced Napoleon to make one of the most difficult decisions of his life: in 1809, after years of trying, Napoleon decided to divorce Joséphine. Although the two continued to love each other deeply, the duty to the Empire and the need to secure a succession led Napoleon to marry Marie Louise of Austria, who bore him a son, Napoleon II.

The divorce was painful for both. At the separation ceremony, Napoleon gave an emotional speech in which he stated that Joséphine would always be his first and greatest passion. Despite their formal separation, Napoleon continued to maintain a close relationship with Joséphine, supporting her financially and visiting her on occasion. Joséphine, for her part, remained loyal to Napoleon until the end of her life.

After her divorce, Joséphine lived at the palace of Malmaison, where she devoted herself to gardening and court life. She died on 29 May 1814, shortly after Napoleon's fall, probably suffering from pneumonia. According to some reports, her last words were: "Bonaparte... Elba", referring to the island where her ex-husband had been exiled.

Napoleon, after being informed of Joséphine's death during his exile in Elba, is said to have been devastated. Despite having had a second marriage and other lovers, Joséphine still held a special place in his heart. On his deathbed in 1821, Napoleon supposedly whispered her name, along with that of his son and that of France.

The romance between Napoleon Bonaparte and Joséphine de Beauharnais was a combination of passion, politics, and tragedy. Their love, although marked by betrayal and pain, is still remembered as one of the most intense and moving in history. The fascination that this relationship continues to generate is a testament to the complexity of human love, especially when it is intertwined with personal ambitions and power. Although their marriage did not last, the emotional and symbolic impact of their relationship has remained etched in human memory as one of the world's most epic love stories.

3. Frida Kahlo and Diego Rivera: A love between art and passion

The relationship between Frida Kahlo and Diego Rivera is one of the most fascinating and complex of the 20th century. More than just a marriage, their union was a mix of art, passion, politics, and pain. Throughout their lives, these two Mexican artists created a legacy that has transcended borders, not only because of the magnitude of their works but also because of the intensity of their romantic relationship. Their love was both tumultuous and deeply inspiring, characterized by its ups and downs, with moments of mutual artistic admiration and periods of infidelity and separation.

Frida Kahlo was born on July 6, 1907, in Coyoacán, Mexico, and from an early age she was marked by physical pain. At the age of six, she contracted poliomyelitis, which left her right leg thinner than her left. At the age of 18, she suffered a bus accident that shattered her spine, ribs, pelvis, and right leg, leaving her with lifelong after-effects. It was during her recovery that Frida began painting, using a special easel that her mother had made for her so that she could paint from her bed.

Frida Kahlo's art is characterized by her surrealist and deeply personal style, in which she portrays the physical and emotional pain she experienced. Throughout her life, Kahlo produced a series of self-portraits that reflect both her suffering and her identity as a Mexican woman. In addition to her painting, Frida was a fervent political activist, committed to communist and nationalist causes in Mexico.

Diego Rivera, born on December 8, 1886, in Guanajuato, Mexico, is widely considered one of the most important artists in Mexico and the world. Rivera was known for his monumental murals, which dealt with historical, social, and political themes, especially focused on the struggle of the working classes and the history of Mexico. After studying in Europe and rubbing shoulders with artists such as Picasso, Rivera returned to Mexico to become the leader of Mexican Muralism, an art movement that promoted the creation of public and accessible art.

Unlike Frida, Rivera was always a prominent public figure, with a strong and expansive personality. He was known not only for his art but for his eventful personal life, marked by his relationship with multiple women and his political activism.

Frida Kahlo met Diego Rivera when she was 22 and he was 42. Frida, who admired Rivera's work since before she met him, sought him out to evaluate her art. Rivera was impressed by Kahlo's talent, describing her as an artist with "energy and honesty." Despite the age difference and Rivera's history as a womanizer, the two began a relationship that was formalized in marriage in 1929.

The bond between Frida and Diego was intense from the beginning. Rivera found in Frida a strong, independent woman with an artistic talent that he could not ignore. Frida, for her part, saw in Rivera a father figure and a mentor, but also a man with whom she fell deeply in love. This marriage was not only a romantic union, but also a creative one, as both influenced each other in their work.

However, from the beginning, the relationship between Frida and Diego was marked by conflicts and challenges. Rivera continued with his infidelities, something that Frida accepted, although it caused her much pain. One of the most painful episodes for Frida was Diego's affair with her younger sister, Cristina Kahlo, an event that deeply affected her emotional and physical health.

Frida, although she deeply loved Diego, also had her affairs, both with men and women. Some of her lovers included figures such as Russian communist politician Leon Trotsky and singer Chavela Vargas. Over the years, their relationship became a whirlwind of emotions, with moments of separation and reconciliation.

In 1939, the couple divorced, mainly due to Diego's multiple infidelities and the emotional strains this caused on Frida. However, just a year later, they remarried. Despite all the difficulties, they never stopped being connected in some way, whether through art, politics, or the mutual affection that always prevailed, even in the darkest of times.

Throughout their relationship, Frida struggled not only with the emotional problems arising from her marriage but also with her constant physical suffering. The after-effects of the accident in her youth worsened over the years, requiring numerous surgeries and long hospital stays. The constant pain and inability to have children deeply affected Frida, themes she captured in many of her most iconic paintings, such as "The Broken Column" and "Henry Ford Hospital."

Diego, although unfaithful, stayed by her side during these difficult episodes. He often suffered too, seeing her bedridden or after her operations. In some ways, their marriage, though tempestuous, was a source of mutual strength in its worst moments.

Throughout their relationship, Frida and Diego shared a deep admiration for each other's work. Frida often said that she had had two accidents in her life: the first, the bus that left her crippled, and the second, Diego. Her love for Rivera was so great that she often said that the emotional pain he caused her was stronger than the physical.

Their legacy as an artistic couple is undeniable. While Diego was a world-renowned muralist, Frida Kahlo was recognized primarily after his death, when her work began to be seen as a symbol of feminism and resilience in the face of adversity. Her art, which reflects her pain, her identity as a Mexican woman, and her relationship with Diego, has made her figure transcend beyond the borders of art.

Frida Kahlo died on July 13, 1954, at the age of 47, due to health complications aggravated by her chronic pain. Diego Rivera, devastated by her death, wrote in his memoirs that he had loved her more than anything in the world and that, without her, his life was meaningless. Rivera died three years later, in 1957.

Frida and Diego's legacy as a couple has endured over time not only because of their art but also because of the complexity of their relationship. Frida Kahlo, with her unwavering strength, has become a feminist icon and a symbol of the fight for personal and national identity. Diego Rivera, for his part, remains one of the most important muralists in history, known for his commitment to social justice and his representation of Mexican history.

The relationship between Frida Kahlo and Diego Rivera is a testament to how love can be both a source of inspiration and pain. Despite the infidelities, disagreements, and health problems they faced, the two found a deep connection in each other that lasted until their final days. Their love, though complicated, has left a legacy of art and culture that continues to influence generations of artists and activists around the world.

4. Pablo Neruda and Matilde Urrutia: The love that inspired 20th-century poetry

The relationship between Pablo Neruda and Matilde Urrutia has been immortalized as one of the most celebrated love stories of the 20th century, in part because the laureate Chilean poet poured his passion into some of his most iconic verses. This love, born in secrecy and marked by personal and political challenges, gave rise to an intense connection that lasted until Neruda died in 1973. Over the years, the story of their relationship has transcended not only for the poetic beauty it inspired but also for the emotional complexities and sacrifices they both faced. As in many great love stories, there was light and shadow in their relationship, with nuances that reflected both the sublime and the problematic of the bond they shared.

Pablo Neruda, whose real name was Ricardo Eliécer Neftalí Reyes Basoalto, was born on July 12, 1904, in Parral, Chile. From a young age, he showed an early talent for poetry and adopted the pseudonym "Pablo Neruda" in honor of the Czech poet Jan Neruda. Throughout his life, Neruda established himself as one of the most important poetic voices of the 20th century, with works covering a wide range of themes, from love and nature to politics and social injustice.

Winner of the Nobel Prize for Literature in 1971, Neruda was known for both his lyrical poetry and his political activism. He was a member of the Chilean Communist Party, a senator, and a diplomat, and he maintained a strong stance in defense of the rights of the oppressed. His public life was marked by his political convictions, but his private life was also intense, especially regarding his romantic relationships.

Matilde Urrutia was born on April 30, 1912, in Chillán, Chile. Before meeting Neruda, Matilde was a prominent opera singer and nurse, known for her work in various artistic settings and her beauty. Although she did not belong to the intellectual or political circles in which Neruda moved, Matilde had a strong personality and independence that made her stand out.

Her meeting with Pablo Neruda marked a turning point in her life. Although Urrutia was initially a secret lover, her presence in the poet's life would be so influential that she would end up becoming his ultimate muse. Matilde became the inspiration behind many of the most passionate and romantic verses that Neruda wrote in his later years.

Pablo Neruda met Matilde Urrutia in the 1940s. At the time, he was married to his second wife, the Argentine painter Delia del Carril, with whom he had a stable relationship, but which had lost its romantic vigor over time. Matilde and Neruda began a clandestine relationship in 1946, while he was still married, and the relationship endured for years under the veil of secrecy. The passion between them was evident, but so was the challenge they faced in keeping their relationship hidden, especially given Neruda's public prominence.

For more than a decade, Matilde and Pablo lived a complicated and often painful relationship. While she suffered the invisibility and pain of being "the other," Neruda was torn between his public life and his private desires. However, the emotional bond between the two was unbreakable, and despite the difficulties, Matilde became the inspiration for one of Neruda's most beautiful collections of love poetry: "Los versos del Capitán." This book, published in 1952, was written in honor of Matilde but was not signed by Neruda at the time to protect his identity and their secret relationship.

Finally, in 1955, Pablo Neruda separated from Delia del Carril and formalized his relationship with Matilde Urrutia. From that moment on, Matilde became not only his sentimental partner but also his caregiver and protector. Over the years, Urrutia played a fundamental role in Neruda's life, helping him manage his health, his schedule, and his commitments.

In 1966, Neruda published "Cien sonetos de amor," one of his most celebrated works, explicitly dedicated to Matilde. In these verses, the poet exalted his love for her, a mature love, full of tenderness and passion. Their relationship became a symbol of love that transcended obstacles, and Matilde was increasingly seen as Neruda's true companion, someone who not only inspired him, but also supported him emotionally and physically.

Neruda's last years of life were marked by illness. In 1970, he was diagnosed with prostate cancer. Matilde became his caregiver, accompanying him during his illness and physical decline. Despite the suffering, the love between them remained strong until the end.

The hardest blow for both came in 1973, with the coup d'état in Chile that overthrew the government of

Salvador Allende. Neruda, always close to Allende and a fervent defender of socialism, was deeply affected by the military coup. His health deteriorated rapidly, and he died on September 23, 1973, in circumstances that still generate controversy today, as some believe he may have been poisoned by agents of Augusto Pinochet's regime.

Matilde Urrutia, devastated by the loss of her husband, dedicated herself to preserving his legacy, publishing her memoirs, and fighting to keep Neruda's figure alive in the cultural imagination, even in times of censorship.

The relationship between Pablo Neruda and Matilde Urrutia has transcended time as one of the great love stories of the 20th century, partly because of the impact it had on Neruda's poetic work and the passion they both shared. Although it was marked by challenges, infidelities, and periods of suffering, the love they professed for each other left an artistic and emotional legacy that continues to inspire new generations.

The positive side of their relationship is evident in the deep emotional and creative connection they shared, one that influenced some of the most notable works of modern poetry. The negative side, on the other hand, is related to the personal sacrifices they both made, especially Matilde, to maintain their relationship, and to the complexities of a love that began in secret.

Ultimately, the love between Neruda and Urrutia is a testament to the human capacity to find beauty and transcendence even amid difficulties, a love that, although imperfect, left an indelible mark on the history of literature and on the hearts of those who read the words the poet wrote for his immortal muse.

5. Anne Boleyn and Henry VIII: Love, Power and Tragedy in English History

The relationship between Anne Boleyn and Henry VIII is one of the most fascinating and tragic stories of the English Renaissance. Their love and subsequent marriage not only changed the course of English history but also symbolized the complex intertwinings between power, politics, and desire. Through their story, human passions, struggles for power, and the fatal consequences of ambition are explored, which has made their relationship transcend time.

Anne Boleyn, born around 1501, was the second daughter of Thomas Boleyn and Lady Elizabeth Howard. From an early age, Anne was educated at the courts of the Netherlands and France, where she acquired not only refinement and elegance but also a strong sense of ambition and desire for power. Upon her return to England, she was introduced to the court of King Henry VIII, where she quickly attracted attention for her beauty, intelligence, and indomitable character.

Anne became a lady-in-waiting to Catherine of Aragon, Henry's first wife, and it was during this time that she began to captivate the king. However, her relationship with Henry was not just a romance; it was a turning point in the religious and political history of England.

Henry VIII, born on June 28, 1491, was the second son of King Henry VII and Elizabeth of York. He ascended the throne in 1509 and initially showed himself to be a capable and attractive monarch. However, his desire for a male heir and his frustration with his wife Catherine's inability to bear him a son began to consume him. Henry's obsession with securing his lineage led him to seek out new alliances and marriages, which would result in a break with the Catholic Church.

Henry's attraction to Anne Boleyn intensified in the 1520s. As their relationship deepened, Henry found himself increasingly frustrated with his marriage to Catherine. Pope Clement VII's refusal to annul his marriage to allow him to marry Anne prompted Henry to take drastic measures. In 1533, Henry broke with the Catholic Church, founded the Church of England, and married Anne, who was pregnant at the time.

Henry and Anne's wedding was held in secret on 25 January 1533, and Anne gave birth to their first child, Elizabeth, on 7 September 1533. Although Elizabeth's birth was celebrated, Henry was desperate for a male heir. Throughout her marriage, Anne suffered several losses, including the death of a son, which increased the strain on her relationship with the king.

Despite her disadvantages, Anne managed to influence court politics. She was an intelligent and charismatic woman who knew how to use her power to support the Protestant Reformation and destabilize the position of

Catherine of Aragon and her daughter, Mary. However, as time went on, Anne's situation became increasingly precarious. The pressure to provide a male heir became a crushing weight, and her relationship with Henry began to deteriorate.

The situation came to a head in 1536 when Anne was arrested on charges of treason, adultery, and incest, many of which are believed to have been fabricated by her enemies at court, including Thomas Cromwell, an advisor to Henry. The trial was a political spectacle that culminated in her being sentenced to death. Anne was executed on 19 May 1536, at the Tower of London, leaving a legacy of tragedy and manipulation in her wake.

The story of Anne Boleyn and Henry VIII has transcended time not only for its dramatic narrative of love and power but also for the social and religious implications of their actions. Their romance has been the subject of numerous literary works, films, and television series, reflecting the enduring interest in their lives and the repercussions of their relationship.

Anne Boleyn has become a symbol of the struggle for power and women's ability to influence the course of history. Her legacy lives on in the figure of her daughter, Elizabeth I, who would become one of the most successful and celebrated queens in English history. Anne's influence extended beyond her lifetime, affecting generations of women and marking a shift in the relationship between the monarch and the church.

The relationship between Anne Boleyn and Henry VIII is one of the most iconic in history, marked by love, ambition, tragedy, and social transformation. Their story is a reminder that while love can be powerful, power struggles, societal expectations, and personal ambitions can often lead to devastating consequences. Anne Boleyn, with her intelligence and determination, became an iconic figure who continues to fascinate and resonate in the collective imagination, symbolizing the complexity of love and power throughout history.

6. Ludwig van Beethoven and the "Unattainable Beloved": A Platonic Love in the Life of the Musical Genius

Ludwig van Beethoven's life is marked not only by his musical brilliance but also by his intense emotional and romantic experiences. One of the most enigmatic and fascinating chapters of his love life is his relationship with his "Unattainable Beloved," a figure who has been the subject of speculation and study over the years. Although the identity of this woman is not known with certainty, her influence on Beethoven's life and work has left an indelible mark, reflecting both the positive and negative side of unrequited love.

Ludwig van Beethoven, born on December 17, 1770, in Bonn, Germany, is considered one of the greatest composers in the history of classical music. From a young age, he showed exceptional musical talent, and his family, especially his father, encouraged him to develop his skills. At age 21, Beethoven moved to

Vienna, where he became a central figure in the transition from Classicism to Romanticism in music.

Throughout his career, Beethoven composed symphonies, concertos, sonatas, and quartets that changed the way music was understood. His works, such as Symphony No. 9 and the Moonlight Sonata, are not only examples of technical genius but are also imbued with deep emotionality. However, Beethoven's personal life was marked by several struggles, including his increasing deafness, which began in his youth and developed into a complete disability in his later years.

One of the most intriguing aspects of Beethoven's life is his relationship with his "Unattainable Beloved," a platonic love who is thought to have influenced his music and emotional life. The identity of this woman has been the subject of debate and speculation. Some biographers suggest that she might have been Josephine Brunsvik, a Hungarian aristocrat whom Beethoven met in his youth and for whom he experienced an intense attraction. Other names that have been proposed include Therese Malfatti and Anna Milder-Hauptmann.

What is certain is that this unrequited, or at least unconsummated, love left a deep mark on the composer's soul. His letters to this woman, especially the famous "Letter to the Unattainable Beloved", are testimonies of his anguish, his desire, and his idealization of love. In this letter, written in 1812, Beethoven expresses his pain and despair at not being able to have the woman he loved. Although it was never sent, it is a display of his vulnerability and deep longings.

Beethoven's love for his "Unattainable Beloved" was not only a personal experience, but also had a significant impact on his music. Many of his compositions from this time are imbued with melancholy and passion that reflects his inner struggle. The famous "Piano Sonata No. 32" and his "String Quartet No. 13" are examples of how his anguish was translated into extraordinary musical beauty.

Beethoven's music often captures the complexity of his emotions – the struggle between desire and despair, hope and sadness. His ability to transform pain into art has resonated deeply with listeners of all generations, making him an icon not only of music but of human expression.

The story of Beethoven and his "Unattainable Beloved" has transcended time for its ability to connect with universal human emotions. Unrequited love, the idealization of love, and the search for beauty in life are themes that resonate across generations. Beethoven, through his music and personal story, has managed to capture the complexity of the human experience.

His love life has been the subject of numerous biographies, films, and literary works that seek to understand the intersection between his personal life and his art. The letter to his "Unattainable Beloved" has become a symbol of the anguish of platonic love and the artist's struggle to find his voice amid despair.

The relationship between Ludwig van Beethoven and his "Unattainable Beloved" is a love story that, although never consummated, left an indelible mark on the composer's life and work. His experience with platonic love reflects the universal struggles of human beings: desire, frustration, and the beauty search. Through his music, Beethoven managed to transform his pain into art, creating works that have endured throughout the centuries and continue to touch the hearts of those who listen to them. His legacy is not only that of a musical genius but also that of a human being who, like everyone, longed to love and be loved.

7. Salvador Dalí and Gala Éluard: The Surrealist Love of an Artistic Genius

The relationship between Salvador Dalí, one of the greatest exponents of surrealism, and Gala Éluard, his muse and life partner, is a story of love, art, and madness that has transcended time. Their intense and tumultuous bond became an integral part of Dalí's life and work, reflecting the complexities of love in the context of creativity and genius.

Salvador Dalí was born on May 11, 1904, in Figueras, Spain. From an early age, he showed an exceptional talent for art, influenced by his studies at the San Fernando School of Fine Arts in Madrid. Dalí joined the surrealist movement in the 1920s, quickly becoming one of its most iconic figures. His distinctive style, characterized by dreamlike imagery and fantastical elements, defied logic and explored the subconscious.

Dalí was also an eccentric and provocative character, known for his pointed mustache, personal style, and erratic behavior. Throughout his career, his work spanned painting, sculpture, film, and photography, and he was noted for his ability to fuse classical technique with avant-garde innovation. His paintings, such as "The Persistence of Memory", are world-renowned, and his influence on modern art is undeniable.

For her part, Gala Éluard, born Eluard on September 7, 1894, in Kazan, Russia, was an enigmatic and charismatic woman who became the muse of several artists, but her most significant relationship was with Dalí. Gala was previously the wife of the surrealist poet Paul Éluard, but her connection with Dalí began in 1929 when they met in Paris. From the first moment, Dalí was captivated by her beauty and her aura.

The relationship between Gala and Dalí was intense and passionate. Gala became not only his lover but also his representative and manager, playing a crucial role in the development of his career. Her support and devotion allowed Dalí to concentrate on his art and explore his creativity without distractions.

The relationship between Dalí and Gala was marked by deep love, but also by possessiveness and jealousy. Gala became the center of his world and his source of inspiration. Gala's influence can be seen in many of Dalí's works, where her figure and essence are intertwined with the artist's dreams and fantasies.

However, their relationship was not without conflict. Gala was known for her strong character and independence, which often led to tensions with Dalí. Despite this, their love endured, and Gala became his wife in 1934, in a ceremony in which both affirmed their mutual devotion.

The love story between Salvador Dalí and Gala Éluard has transcended for its uniqueness and the emotional intensity it represented. Gala became the muse who inspired some of Dalí's most memorable works, and her presence in his personal and artistic life is undeniable. The legacy of their love is reflected in the way Dalí addressed themes of passion, desire, and madness in his work.

Furthermore, the relationship between Dalí and Gala has been the subject of numerous studies, films, and biographies, cementing its place in the history of art and artistic relationships. The image of the couple, often portrayed in the press and popular culture, has perpetuated the notion of the artist and his muse as an inseparable combination.

The positive side of Dalí and Gala's relationship is manifested in the creative drive that Gala provided Dalí. Her unconditional love and support allowed him to explore his art and experiment with new ideas. Gala was a stabilizing force in the artist's life, and her influence was reflected in the recognition and success that Dalí achieved in the art world.

Furthermore, their relationship challenged the conventions of the time, showing that love and art can coexist in a unique form of expression. The combination of Dalí's creative force and Gala's vibrant personality resulted in a synergy that propelled surrealism and left an indelible mark on art history.

The negative side of their relationship is also worth mentioning. Despite the devotion they shared, the relationship between Dalí and Gala was plagued by jealousy and tension. Dalí's possessive nature sometimes became oppressive, leading to conflict between the two. Gala, with her free spirit, longed for independence but also faced the pressure of being the artist's muse.

Furthermore, the relationship was affected by Dalí's fame and notoriety. As he achieved international success, public attention and scrutiny of his personal life increased, leading to tensions in their relationship. Gala became a target of rumors and speculation, further complicating their bond.

Gala passed away on June 10, 1982, and her death deeply affected Dalí. The loss of his muse left a void in his life and his art, and although he continued to create, his work never again had the same spark as when Gala was by his side. Their relationship remains a symbol of the love between a creative genius and his muse, and their legacy lives on in the way the two intertwined in art and life.

Salvador Dalí, meanwhile, died on January 23, 1989, in Figueres, Spain, from cardiac arrest. He was 84 years old.

The story of Dalí and Gala reminds us that love, with all its complexities, can be a powerful force that drives artists to explore the depths of their creativity, challenging norms and embracing the madness of life and art. Their legacy lives on in the masterpieces they created together and in the collective memory of those who are drawn to the beauty of love and art.

8. Heloise and Abelard: A forbidden love that transcended history

The story of Heloise and Abelard is one of the most tragic and romantic love stories of the Middle Ages, a testament to how love can defy social and religious norms. Their relationship has endured through the centuries, inspiring poets, writers, and philosophers due to its emotional depth and the hardships they faced. The lives of these two characters stand out not only for their passionate love but also for their contribution to philosophical and literary thought.

Peter Abelard was born in 1079 in Pallet, a small town in the Nantes region of France. From a young age, he displayed a brilliant mind and became one of the most influential philosophers and theologians of his time. Abelard was known for his rational approach and skill for debate, which allowed him to attract numerous students and followers. He excelled in the use of logic and dialectics, which led him to be one of the first thinkers to question the established doctrines of the church.

His most famous work, "Sic et Non," is an essay in which he presents a series of contradictions in sacred texts and other religious authorities, promoting critical thinking and questioning. His revolutionary approach attracted attention but also earned him enemies at a time when orthodoxy was the norm.

In turn, Heloise of Argenteuil, born around 1100, was an exceptionally intelligent and cultured young woman, niece of Canon Fulbert, who educated her. Her intelligence and talent distinguished her in an era when women had limited access to education. Heloise became a well-educated woman and began to study the works of the philosophers and theologians of her time, which led her to be a notable figure in the intellectual court.

In 1120, Abelard met Heloise, who was living on the Cité Islands with her uncle Fulbert. At the time, she was probably in her early twenties and Abelard decided to seduce her and offered his uncle to be her tutor. At the time, she was known for being a brilliant scholar and for her great knowledge of Latin, Greek, and Hebrew.

The intellectual connection between the two quickly developed into a romantic attraction, and soon their relationship transcended simple academic friendship.

The romance blossomed in an atmosphere of secrecy and passion, defying the social and religious norms of their time. Abelard caught between his desire for Heloise and his commitment to intellectual and religious life, became a fervent and passionate lover.

However, their forbidden love did not go unnoticed. When the relationship became apparent, Heloise's uncle Fulbert felt betrayed and offended. They eloped, had a son who died shortly after, and endured countless hardships in hiding. They were caught sometime later. In an act of revenge, Fulberto ordered Abelard to be castrated. This event marked a turning point in their lives and ended their physical relationship.

The story of Heloísa and Abelard has transcended for its tragic narrative of love, desire, and suffering. The duality of their relationship, which encompassed passion and intellectuality, has resonated throughout the centuries. Their correspondence, in which deeply emotional letters were exchanged, reflects the struggle between their love and social expectations, showing the pain and loss they experienced.

The writings of Abelard and Heloise have been studied for their emotional depth and philosophical relevance. The couple are remembered not only as lovers but also as intellectual figures who challenged the norms of their time, contributing to the development of medieval thought.

The positive side of the relationship between Heloise and Abelard lies in the intellectual connection they share. They were both deep thinkers and their interactions fostered an exchange of ideas that enriched their lives. Heloise, despite the limitations of her time, became a powerful voice in the field of critical thought, thanks to her relationship with Abelard.

The correspondence between the two has also left an invaluable literary legacy. The letters they exchanged are considered masterpieces of love and passion, expressing their feelings eloquently and movingly. These writings have inspired generations of readers and writers, keeping their love alive throughout history.

However, Heloise and Abelard's love was marked by tragedy and suffering. Abelard's castration and the forced separation that followed led to a life of pain and disappointment for both. Heloise retired to a convent, where she became an abbess, while Abelard devoted himself to monastic life, marking the end of their romantic relationship.

The tragedy of their story highlights the difficulties they faced as lovers in a world that did not accept their union. The forced separation and the suffering they endured are a reminder of how social and religious norms can oppress love and happiness.

Despite the challenges, the story of Heloise and Abelard remains a powerful symbol of true love and the struggle for emotional and intellectual freedom. Their life and relationships have become a source of inspiration for poets, philosophers, and artists throughout the centuries. The duality of their love, filled with passion and suffering, has resonated in popular culture and has been reinterpreted in various ways.

Their legacy lives on in literature, philosophy, and love history. Heloísa and Abelardo have become archetypes of tragic lovers, reminding us that true love, despite adversity, can defy time and convention. Their story remains a reflection of desire, reason, and the struggles faced by those who love deeply and authentically.

9. Karl Marx and Jenny von Westphalen: A Revolutionary Love

The relationship between Karl Marx and Jenny von Westphalen is one of the most passionate and enduring love stories in modern history. Despite living amidst great economic and political hardship, the marriage between Marx and Jenny was a central pillar in the life of the German philosopher. Their love story transcended social barriers, economic pressures, and political persecution, and has endured as a testament to commitment, loyalty, and mutual support in a context of adversity.

Karl Marx was born on May 5, 1818, in Trier, Prussia (now Germany). Marx would become one of the most influential philosophers in history, known for his development of historical materialism and his theories on class struggle, captured in works such as "The Communist Manifesto" and "Das Kapital." Throughout his life, Marx fought not only against the social injustices he denounced but also against the personal and economic hardships that marked his existence.

Despite the turmoil of his intellectual and political life, Marx found in Jenny von Westphalen an unwavering companion, a woman of great strength who shared his ideals and supported him in his most difficult moments.

Johanna Bertha Julie Jenny von Westphalen, born on February 12, 1814, in Salzwedel, Prussia, came from an aristocratic family. Her father, Baron Ludwig von Westphalen, was a high-ranking Prussian official with progressive ideas who influenced Jenny's upbringing. Despite being educated in a privileged environment, Jenny always showed inclinations for philosophy, politics, and social causes.

From an early age, Jenny was known for her beauty, intelligence, and independent spirit. When she met Karl Marx, the two shared a deep intellectual and emotional connection, despite class differences. For a woman from the Prussian aristocracy, engagement with a man like Marx, who was without financial resources and had revolutionary ideas, represented a bold and unusual act in her time.

The relationship between Karl Marx and Jenny von Westphalen began when they were both young in Trier. Despite the social differences between them, they became secretly engaged in 1836, when Jenny was 22 and Marx 18. This engagement was a challenge to the social norms of the time, as an aristocratic woman was expected to marry within her class.

After several years of engagement and separation due to Marx's studies, they were married on 19 June 1843 in Kreuznach. From that moment on, Jenny became not only Marx's wife but also his closest collaborator. Although she was neither a writer nor a theorist in the formal sense, Jenny played a crucial role in Marx's life, helping to edit and organize his writings and providing him with constant emotional support.

Throughout their marriage, the couple had seven children, although only three of them survived to adulthood. The Marxes' family life was marked by poverty and instability. They lived in very precarious conditions, particularly during their exile in London, where they suffered financial hardship and the loss of several children. However, their love and commitment to each other never wavered.

Over the years, Jenny was a figure of unwavering strength for Marx. Not only did she take care of the management of the household, but she also played an important role in her husband's career, helping to correct manuscripts and supporting his intellectual endeavors. Marx affectionately nicknamed her "my baroness", acknowledging his wife's nobility in both character and origin.

Jenny also shared her husband's revolutionary ideas, although she never became directly involved in politics. She was a companion who not only supported him personally but also politically and ideologically, being one of his most critical readers and one of the first to share his concerns about the social problems of the time.

Furthermore, despite the economic hardships they faced, Jenny's love and devotion to Marx did not fade. Her commitment remained steadfast even when her life was marked by tragedy and exile. She often sacrificed her well-being and that of her children for the cause of her husband, displaying a loyalty and dedication that few marriages have known.

Despite their emotional closeness, Jenny's life with Marx was fraught with sacrifice and suffering. The chronic poverty that dogged them, especially during their years in London, was a crushing burden for Jenny. She often found herself without the basic resources to care for her children, and the death of several of them was a devastating blow to both.

Jenny's dedication to Marx also entailed a life of personal renunciation. Although she came from an aristocratic family, she was forced to endure extreme poverty and constant uncertainty. Her role as wife and mother often overshadowed any personal ambition she might have had, and Marx's intellectual work always came first.

Furthermore, the relationship had its tensions. Although Marx loved her deeply, he is also known to have had an extramarital affair with his housekeeper, Helene Demuth, who gave birth to a son, Frederick Demuth, in 1851. This fact was a painful blow to Jenny, although the affair was kept secret from most of her contemporaries and did not affect her loyalty to Marx.

The love story between Karl Marx and Jenny von Westphalen has transcended time because it represents an example of love and unwavering commitment in extremely difficult circumstances. Their marriage was a union of ideals, where Jenny played a crucial role in the life of one of the most influential thinkers in modern history.

Jenny has been remembered as Marx's companion and emotional support, but her importance goes far beyond being just "the wife of." She was an intelligent, strong, and courageous woman, who fought alongside her husband in his quest to change the world. Despite the hardships, her love endured, and her sacrifice and loyalty to Marx and his revolutionary cause have made her an inspiring figure.

10. John Lennon and Yoko Ono: A love that broke barriers

The relationship between John Lennon and Yoko Ono is one of the most famous and controversial in contemporary history. Their story of love, art, and activism transcended the boundaries of music and popular culture, marking a before and after in the public lives of both. While many see it as a relationship that personified the power of love and creativity, others consider it a catalyst for tensions, especially within The Beatles. Despite criticism and controversy, their personal and artistic bond endures in the collective memory as a symbol of rebellion, change, and mutual commitment.

John Lennon was born on October 9, 1940, in Liverpool, England. From a young age, he showed an inclination towards music and eventually became the co-founder and one of the most iconic members of The Beatles, the band that revolutionized pop music in the

1960s. Lennon, along with Paul McCartney, wrote some of the band's biggest hits, becoming a musical legend.

Although his success with The Beatles was monumental, Lennon was also a man in search of personal meaning and a new way to express his thoughts and emotions. At the height of his career, he met Yoko Ono, a Japanese conceptual artist, which would change his life forever.

Yoko Ono, born on February 18, 1933, in Tokyo, Japan, came from an aristocratic family. From a young age, Ono was noted for her independent mind and inclination towards the arts. She moved to New York in the 1950s and immersed herself in the world of avant-garde art and performance art. Her work challenged traditional art norms, and her creative ideas were often seen as radical and misunderstood.

When she met Lennon in 1966 at an exhibition of his work in London, they felt an immediate emotional and intellectual connection. Yoko had been married before, as had Lennon, but a bond developed between them that soon transcended any previous commitments.

The relationship between John Lennon and Yoko Ono began clandestinely, as Lennon was married to Cynthia Powell, with whom he had a son, Julian Lennon. However, the attraction between Lennon and Ono was so strong that John left his marriage to be with Yoko. They married on March 20, 1969, in Gibraltar, and from then on, they became one of the most public and media-friendly couples of the 20th century.

Their marriage was not simply a romantic union; it was also an artistic and political collaboration. From the beginning, John and Yoko used their relationship as a platform for their pacifist and social activism ideas. One of their most symbolic acts was their "Bed-In" in March 1969, a non-violent protest for world peace, in which the two stayed in their hotel bed while receiving the press to talk about peace. The event attracted international media attention and consolidated their image as activists.

Yoko's influence on Lennon's life was profound. She helped him expand his artistic horizons, moving him away from the commercial structures of The Beatles and leading him towards more abstract and experimental forms of expression. His music, from then on, was marked by a more personal and introspective approach, as demonstrated by the album "John Lennon/Plastic Ono Band."

The positive side of the relationship between John Lennon and Yoko Ono lies in the creative and personal freedom that both found in their union. Lennon, who had lived a life of constant media attention and professional pressures within The Beatles, found in Yoko a refuge and a partner who understood him on an artistic and emotional level. Yoko was instrumental in helping Lennon explore his individuality, pushing him to take creative risks and move away from mainstream pop music.

Their relationship was also a powerful symbol of freedom and transgression. In an era when interracial relationships and unconventional unions were subject to prejudice, Lennon and Ono challenged those barriers. Together, they promoted ideals of peace and love that resonated with a generation seeking social and political change, particularly during the Vietnam War. Their famous song "Give Peace a Chance" became an anthem of the anti-war movement.

In addition, their artistic relationship was fruitful, collaborating on numerous occasions. Their album "Double Fantasy," released in 1980 shortly before Lennon's death, was a testament to their creative collaboration, merging their artistic visions into a musical dialogue.

However, the relationship between John Lennon and Yoko Ono was not without controversy and tension. For many Beatles fans, Yoko was seen as a divisive figure, who was partly blamed for the band's breakup in 1970. Although the reasons for the Beatles' dissolution were complex and multiple, Yoko's influence on Lennon and her growing interest in artistic and personal projects away from the band fueled these perceptions.

Furthermore, the relationship was marked by moments of emotional instability and separation. In 1973, Lennon and Ono went through a crisis that resulted in a brief period of breakup known as Lennon's "Lost Weekend", in which he maintained a relationship with his assistant, May Pang, for approximately 18 months. Although Lennon and Yoko reconciled in 1975, this period revealed the difficulties and tensions in their relationship.

Another negative aspect was the constant media exposure and criticism that both received, especially Yoko. The press and many of Lennon's fans viewed Yoko as an outsider in the world of rock, attacking her both for her influence on Lennon and for her art, which many considered strange or incomprehensible. Yoko was a victim of racism and sexism and was often portrayed as the villain of the story.

Despite the controversies, the relationship between John Lennon and Yoko Ono has endured as one of the most iconic romances in modern culture. Their love and artistic collaboration broke down traditional barriers of what was expected of a famous couple. Together, they promoted art as a tool for social change and explored the intersection between music, activism, and love.

Following Lennon's assassination on December 8, 1980, Yoko continued his legacy, keeping his memory and message of peace alive. Their relationship has become a symbol of how love and art can merge to challenge the status quo and strive for higher ideals. Although they were often misunderstood or criticized, their union is still remembered as an example of mutual commitment, both personally and artistically.

11. Marilyn Monroe and Arthur Miller: A relationship between fame and intellectuality

The relationship between Marilyn Monroe and Arthur Miller was one of the most unexpected and complex of the golden age of Hollywood. At first glance, they represented opposite worlds: she, the ultimate icon of beauty and glamour on the screen, and he, one of the most respected playwrights in the United States, known for his deep introspection on the human condition. However, their relationship, which ended in marriage, was an attempt by both to find in the other an emotional refuge and an intellectual connection. Although it ended in separation, their love story has endured as an example of the tension between fame and the search for meaning beyond the spotlight.

Marilyn Monroe, born Norma Jeane Mortenson on June 1, 1926, in Los Angeles, California, is remembered as one of the greatest sex symbols in the history of cinema. Behind her "dumb blonde" image, Monroe was a woman of depth, struggling with insecurities and a past full of difficulties, including the absence of her father and her mother's mental problems. Although she projected an image of confidence in her films and front of the cameras, Marilyn was constantly seeking a deeper validation than that offered by the public and the film industry.

Monroe was aware that many saw her only as an object of desire, but she wanted more than anything to be recognized as a serious actress. This led her to study at the Actor's Studio in New York, where she became more involved in theater and the search for a deeper artistic sense in her career. It was in this context that she met Arthur Miller, a man who represented for her everything she lacked: intellect, depth, and a perspective on the world that went beyond the superficial gloss of Hollywood.

For his part, Arthur Miller was born on October 17, 1915, in New York, and from an early age, he stood out for his ability to write about the internal tensions of human beings and the pressures of society. His most recognized works, such as "Death of a Salesman" (1949) and "The Witches of Salem" (1953), address themes such as failure, guilt, and the search for identity in a world full of impossible expectations.

For Miller, art was a way to reflect on the internal struggles of human beings, and his vision of the world was much more intellectual and critical than that of Hollywood. Although he was already a respected man in literary and theatrical circles, his life changed dramatically when he began his relationship with Monroe, a woman who symbolized everything he criticized in terms of fame and superficiality.

Monroe and Miller met in 1951 when she was beginning to gain notoriety in Hollywood. However, it was in 1955, when Monroe was already an established star, that they met again and began a serious relationship. By this time, Monroe was tired of superficial relationships and constant press scrutiny, while Miller had ended their marriage of more than a decade. They both saw each other as an escape from their respective worlds.

Marilyn saw in Arthur an intellectual man, different from the men she had met in Hollywood. He treated her with respect and admiration for her mind, not just her beauty. For his part, Miller found in Monroe a much more complex woman than the world saw, someone who was desperately seeking something deeper than fame.

They married on June 29, 1956, in a private ceremony in New York, and later in a more formal Jewish wedding. At the time, their marriage was a topic of global interest, as few could understand how a movie star like Monroe and an intellectual playwright like Miller could have formed such a strong bond.
At first, Monroe and Miller's marriage seemed idyllic. He became her emotional support, and she, his muse. Miller wrote the script for "The Misfits" (1961), a film tailor-made for Marilyn, which would be her last major film performance. However, pressures began to wear down the relationship.

Monroe suffered from depression, addictions, and a deep insecurity about her worth beyond her public image. Meanwhile, Miller faced his internal struggle, feeling the weight of the expectations of being the husband of one of the most famous women in the world. Their relationship began to crack under the constant scrutiny of the press and the pressures of Hollywood, which did not stop putting Monroe in the spotlight for her problems.

The loss of a pregnancy in 1957 was a hard blow for Monroe, who always wanted to be a mother. This fact, combined with the pressure of remaining a star in Hollywood and her mental health problems, began to distance the couple. Miller, though trying to be supportive, became overwhelmed by the situation.

Their relationship slowly began to fall apart, and tensions between the two became more apparent during the filming of "The Misfits." Miller became emotionally distant, while Monroe sank deeper into her mental health and substance abuse issues.

The relationship between Marilyn Monroe and Arthur Miller was rooted in a mutual desire to be more than their circumstances. Monroe saw in Miller the possibility of transcending her public image and being respected as a serious actress, while Miller saw in Monroe a deeply complex woman, beyond the sex symbol the world perceived her to be.

During their time together, they both challenged each other intellectually and emotionally. Miller was a figure who helped Monroe deepen her love of literature, politics, and art. On the other hand, Monroe was a muse for Miller, inspiring him to explore new dimensions of human nature in his writing.

The dark side of their relationship was the constant tension between Monroe's desire to be seen as more than just a movie star and the demands that this placed on their marriage. Monroe, who suffered from deep insecurities, found in Miller someone who, while loving her, also withdrew from her at critical moments. In addition, public pressure and Monroe's addiction put an immense emotional burden on both, bringing them to a breaking point.

Miller's professional success contrasted with Monroe's struggles to remain emotionally stable, which created an imbalance in the relationship. Although they tried to save their marriage, their differences and Marilyn's mental health problems led to their divorce in 1961.

The relationship between Marilyn Monroe and Arthur Miller has transcended time because it represents the union of two emblematic figures of their respective worlds: the glamour of Hollywood and the intellectual depth of the theater. Their story reflects how relationships between people from different worlds can be both enriching and devastating.

For many, their relationship symbolizes Monroe's struggle to be more than a beauty icon, while for others, it is a testament to how even the love between two brilliant people can succumb to external pressures and internal battles.

After their divorce, Monroe continued to struggle with her demons until her tragic death in 1962. Miller, for his part, remained a prominent figure in the theater, though his time with Monroe left a deep mark on him. "The Misfits," the film he wrote for her, remains a key work in understanding both their relationship and the impact Monroe had on his creative life.

12. Virginia Woolf and Vita Sackville-West: A Literary and Emotional Love That Defied Conventions

The relationship between Virginia Woolf and Vita Sackville-West is one of the most fascinating and influential love stories of the 20th century, especially within the literary context. Although both were married women and maintained their public lives in heterosexual marriages, their connection was deep, intellectual, and emotional. This bond transcended the boundaries of simple romance, significantly influencing Woolf's work and cementing its place in history as a relationship that defied the conventions of the time. Through this relationship, not only the boundaries of romantic love were explored, but also the dynamics of power, identity, and artistic creation.

Virginia Woolf, born on January 25, 1882, in London, was one of the most influential writers of her time, known for works such as "Mrs. Dalloway" (1925), "To the Lighthouse" (1927) and "Orlando" (1928). Woolf is celebrated for her innovations in narrative style, especially interior monologue and stream of consciousness, which she used to explore human psychology and the most intimate experiences of her characters.

Throughout her life, Woolf struggled with bouts of depression and mental health issues, which is often reflected in the emotional depth and psychological sensitivity of her writing. She was married to Leonard Woolf, an editor and writer who was a fundamental support to her, both in her personal life and in her literary career. However, their marriage, although strong in terms of companionship, did not prevent Virginia Woolf from exploring emotional relationships beyond traditional boundaries, especially in the complex relationship she had with Vita Sackville-West.

Vita Sackville-West, born on 9 March 1892 in Knole House, Kent, was a member of the British aristocracy. Although she came from a noble family, Vita was also a noted writer, poet, and gardener. Her literary work includes novels such as The Edwardians (1930) and All Passion Spent (1931), but she is also remembered for her intense personal life, which challenged the gender and sexual norms of the time.

Sackville-West was married to the diplomat and writer Harold Nicolson, with whom she had an open relationship. They shared a mutual understanding of sexual inclinations and extramarital affairs. While Vita had relationships with other women, Harold also had relationships with men. Their marriage was a source of stability at a time when such arrangements were considered radical, and they were both supportive of each other's artistic careers.

Virginia Woolf and Vita Sackville-West met in 1922 through common literary circles, as they were both leading figures in the Bloomsbury Group, an elite group of intellectuals and artists who challenged the social norms of their time. Vita, ten years younger than Virginia, was fascinated by Woolf's mind, while Virginia was drawn to Vita's security and her fascinating life, full of adventure and deviations from convention.

Their relationship began as a friendship that soon became intimate and romantic. Throughout their relationship, they sent each other letters filled with affection, humor, and personal confessions. These letters, many of which survive, are evidence of the strong emotional bond between them. Although their relationship was not always sexual, it was deeply intimate, and Vita became a source of inspiration for Woolf.

The best-known and most enduring aspect of the relationship between Woolf and Sackville-West is the novel "Orlando" (1928). This book, which is one of Woolf's most experimental, was written as a kind of love letter to Vita. The work tells the story of a young nobleman who lives through several centuries, changing sex in the process. Orlando is a celebration of gender fluidity and the immutability of love, regardless of time or body.

The character of Orlando is inspired by Vita, both in her physical appearance and in her gender ambiguity, which challenges expectations of traditional femininity. In this work, Woolf explores the power of love and identity beyond conventional boundaries, reflecting her unique relationship with Sackville-West. For many, "Orlando" is not only a literary masterpiece but also a testament to how love between two people can be transformative, creatively stimulating, and revolutionary.

The positive side of the relationship between Virginia Woolf and Vita Sackville-West is undeniable in the impact it had on the lives and work of both. Woolf found in Vita a source of joy, admiration, and emotional freedom. Their relationship not only provided her with emotional comfort in times of hardship but was also a creative spark that led to the creation of one of her most significant works, "Orlando."

Vita, for her part, was deeply influenced by Woolf's brilliance. They both shared a deep admiration for each other's intellectual achievements, and although their personalities were very different—Vita more practical and adventurous, and Virginia more introspective and emotional—they found in their relationship a perfect combination of emotional and mental stimulation. The fact that both women were married to men who understood and accepted this relationship was also a testament to the times and the progressive circle in which they moved.

The negative side of the relationship focused on the personal and emotional differences that eventually created distance between them. Vita, who had a more emotionally stable nature, did not always understand the depths of Woolf's inner struggles, as Woolf suffered from bouts of severe depression and mental anguish. On the other hand, Woolf sometimes felt that Vita did not share her emotional intensity, and while the relationship was intense at the time, it began to cool over time.

Furthermore, the relationship was always limited by social conventions and both women's marriages, which prevented it from being more than an emotional and artistic connection, at least publicly. As their lives took different paths, the romantic relationship dissolved, although they maintained a lasting friendship until Woolf died in 1941.

The relationship between Virginia Woolf and Vita Sackville-West has transcended time not only for its unconventional nature but also for the impact it had on literature and the depiction of love between women at a time when such relationships were rarely openly discussed. Their bond was more than just a romance: it was an artistic and emotional collaboration that produced a lasting work of literature and showed the world that love does not have to conform to traditional norms to be powerful and meaningful.

"Orlando" remains one of the most important texts on gender and sexual fluidity and is seen as a manifesto of love's ability to transcend traditional categories. The relationship between Woolf and Sackville-West is remembered as an example of how deep emotional connections can change lives and create art that lasts beyond the time in which it was conceived.

13. Alfred de Musset and George Sand: A tempestuous love that marked romantic literature

The relationship between Alfred de Musset and George Sand is one of the most passionate, stormy, and talked about of the 19th century. These two literary giants of French Romanticism lived a romance full of ups and downs, marked by love, mutual admiration, jealousy, and betrayal. Their relationship has transcended time not only for its intensity but also for the profound impact it had on their respective literary works. This love, with its mix of creativity and suffering, personifies the ideals of Romanticism: the exaltation of emotions, individual freedom, and the transformative power of love.

George Sand, born Amandine Aurore Lucile Dupin on July 1, 1804, was a prolific writer, known for her novels, essays, and letters that challenged the conventions of the time. Sand, who adopted a male pseudonym so that she could publish and be taken seriously in the male-dominated literary world, is considered one of the most influential female authors of the 19th century. Her work addresses themes such as personal freedom, social justice, and women's rights.

In addition to her literature, George Sand was known for her unconventional lifestyle. She often wore men's clothing, smoked in public, and lived her life with an independence that contrasted with the standards of the time. Sand had several love affairs with prominent men in the worlds of art and politics, but it was her affair with Alfred de Musset that captured the public's imagination.

Alfred de Musset, born on 11 December 1810, was a French poet, playwright, and novelist, and one of the leading exponents of Romanticism. His work is imbued with a deep sense of melancholy, passion, and despair, often reflecting his struggles with love and disappointment. Musset was known for his bohemian lifestyle, his penchant for excess, and his extreme emotional sensitivity.

Before meeting George Sand, Musset had already written some of his best works, but his relationship with Sand led him to write texts that went down in history as the most intense and painful of his career. Throughout his life, Musset searched for ideal love, but he was also a man of fluctuating desires, which turned his relationship with Sand into an emotional battlefield.

George Sand and Alfred de Musset met in 1833 when Sand was already an established author and Musset an emerging figure in romantic literature. From the beginning, their relationship was marked by an intense mutual attraction. Sand, 6 years older than Musset, was impressed by the poet's youth, vitality, and talent, while Musset was captivated by Sand's intelligence and free spirit. They soon began a romance that became one of the most tumultuous and talked about of the era.

In 1834, the couple traveled to Venice, hoping to find peace and renew their love away from the pressures of Paris. However, this trip proved to be the climax of their relationship and the beginning of the end. During their stay in the city, Musset became seriously ill, putting a strain on the relationship. Sand cared for him devotedly, but also began to grow close to his attending physician, Dr. Pagello, which aroused Musset's jealousy.

Musset, whose physical and emotional health was deteriorating, spiraled into mistrust, jealousy, and despair. Eventually, the relationship began to fall apart. Although both attempted to reconcile, the tension between them was unsustainable. Musset returned to Paris before Sand, who remained in Venice with Pagello for some time.

Upon their return to Paris, the relationship between Musset and Sand continued intermittently. They drifted apart, reconciled, and separated again on several occasions, in a dynamic filled with drama, passionate letters, and unfulfilled promises. However, their love ended definitively in 1835, when both decided that their relationship was too harmful to continue.

Despite the pain, the breakup was a source of inspiration for both Musset and Sand. Musset, deeply affected by the end of their affair, channeled his anguish into his work "The Confession of a Child of the Century" (1836), a semi-autobiographical novel describing his disillusionment with love and the world in general. In this work, Musset portrays the conflict between romantic idealism and the harsh reality of life and relationships.

For her part, George Sand also reflected on their relationship in her novel "Elle et Lui" (1859), a narrative about her affair with Musset from her perspective. In this work, Sand defended her position and questioned Musset's immature and self-destructive behavior, while also acknowledging the intensity of her love for him. In response, Musset's brother Paul published "Lui et Elle," a version of events that supported Alfred, adding further controversy to the already complex legacy of this relationship.

The love story between Alfred de Musset and George Sand has transcended time for its symbolism within the Romantic movement. They embodied the archetype of passionate lovers whose relationship, although destructive, gave rise to a literary work of great significance. The dynamics of their relationship, filled with love, jealousy, betrayal, and pain, continue to fascinate readers and scholars who see in them an example of how art can flourish while suffering.

Their romance was also significant because it represented the struggle between idealized romantic aspirations and the practical realities of love in everyday life. Musset and Sand, with their contrasting personalities, personified that struggle, which is one of the great themes of Romanticism: the tension between the human desire for emotional transcendence and the inherent limitations of relationships.

The relationship between Alfred de Musset and George Sand was a whirlwind of emotions that left an indelible mark on the history of literature. Their love, full of passion and conflict, became the driving force behind some of both writers' most important works, and though their relationship was brief and painful, it has endured as a symbol of the excesses and challenges of romantic love. Their story remains a reminder that love, at its most intense, can be both a source of creation and destruction, a central theme of Romanticism and the human experience in general.

14. El Cid and Jimena Díaz: A story of love, loyalty and legend

The relationship between Rodrigo Díaz de Vivar, known as El Cid Campeador, and Jimena Díaz is one of the most iconic love stories in the history of Spain, which has transcended not only for Rodrigo's military and political greatness but also for the commitment and loyalty that both showed in times of difficulties and adversity. This relationship, immortalized in the Cantar de Mio Cid and Spanish popular tradition, represents the bond between love, devotion, and duty in a time of wars, betrayals, and reconquests.

Rodrigo Díaz de Vivar was born in 1043 in the small town of Vivar, near Burgos, in the Kingdom of Castile. Coming from a noble family, he stood out as a skilled warrior and military strategist, earning respect and fame in the courts of Castile and Aragon. During his lifetime, Rodrigo served as a knight under Kings Sancho II and Alfonso VI of León and Castile, taking part in numerous military campaigns during the Reconquista, the process of recovering territories occupied by the Muslims in the Iberian Peninsula. However, his life was marked by a series of exiles and clashes with the monarchy, which led him to fight under his banner and earn the title of El Cid Campeador.

The figure of El Cid was very complex. Although he was known as a Christian hero of the Reconquista, he also maintained alliances with Muslim lords when politics and circumstances demanded it, demonstrating his pragmatism and ability to navigate a world of political intrigue and constant change.

At his side, Jimena Díaz was a noblewoman, daughter of Diego Fernández de Oviedo, an influential count of the Kingdom of León, and was related to the royal family. She married Rodrigo Díaz de Vivar sometime around the year 1074. Although relatively little is known about her life before the marriage, what is clear is that Jimena embodied the virtues of a medieval wife: loyalty, devotion, and strength.

Jimena and Rodrigo's marriage was not solely a political union. Although marriages of the period were often motivated by reasons of convenience or alliance, the bond between them was characterized by deep mutual devotion, especially visible during the most difficult times, such as Rodrigo's banishments and long separations due to military campaigns.

The Cantar de Mio Cid, the great medieval Spanish epic poem, describes in detail the relationship between El Cid and Jimena. Although the poem is a literary work and not a historical document in its entirety, it reflects the respect and admiration that Jimena felt for her husband, as well as Rodrigo's love and concern for her and her family.

One of the most moving episodes in the Cantar is the banishment of El Cid by order of King Alfonso VI. Before leaving, Rodrigo says goodbye to Jimena and his daughters in a moment full of emotion, praying to God to take care of them. The farewell symbolizes not only the love between husband and wife but also the sacrifice that both are willing to make in the name of duty and honor. Jimena, for her part, accepts her fate with courage, trusting that Rodrigo will triumph and return one day.

Over the years, Jimena and Rodrigo suffered multiple separations due to El Cid's military campaigns, but their relationship remained strong. Jimena was not only a passive spectator in her husband's life; when Rodrigo took Valencia in 1094 and became the lord of the city, Jimena accompanied him and lived there with him, taking an active role in the administration of her new territory.

The secret of the relationship between El Cid and Jimena lies in the unwavering loyalty and deep love they professed for each other, even in the darkest of times. Despite the hardships, Jimena remained by his side, demonstrating impressive inner strength. Through the challenges of exile, war, and prolonged separations, their marriage symbolized a true partnership of companionship and sacrifice.

In addition, Jimena also displayed a high degree of autonomy. Following El Cid's death in 1099, she assumed control of Valencia, ruling the city in his name until she was forced to leave in 1102 when the Almoravids attacked the city. Her role in the defense of Valencia reflects her leadership ability and firmness, characteristics that, in the context of the time, distinguished her from many other noble women.

Nevertheless, their love was tested time and again. Despite their passion, Jimena and Rodrigo were separated for long periods due to El Cid's military campaigns. These absences forced Jimena to live in uncertainty and solitude, something that, according to some accounts, may have caused emotional pain to both her and her children.

Furthermore, the fact that the marriage was affected by the political tensions of the time, such as Rodrigo's banishment and the shifting alliances between Christian and Muslim kingdoms, probably made their relationship even more difficult. Although their love and mutual loyalty were strong, external circumstances often put their bond to the test.

The relationship between El Cid and Jimena has transcended through the centuries for being a symbol of love and loyalty in times of conflict. The epic poem Cantar de Mio Cid has played an important role in the mythologization of this relationship, presenting it as an example of virtue, honor, and sacrifice. Their love has been depicted in countless literary works, paintings, and film productions, establishing itself as one of the most iconic love stories in Spanish culture.

The image of Jimena as a faithful wife who supports her husband in times of adversity has resonated throughout history, making her a model of feminine virtue in medieval and Renaissance traditions. At the same time, the figure of El Cid has been mythologized as the perfect hero, not only on the battlefield but also as a devoted and protective husband.

15. Clara and Robert Schumann: A Life of Love, Music and Genius

The relationship between Clara Wieck Schumann and Robert Schumann is one of the most fascinating in the history of classical music. It was a union marked by artistic creativity, mutual support, personal tragedy, and the challenges of living in an era that limited the role of women. The story of their love has transcended time not only for its intensity and complicity but also for the fusion of their lives as artists, where music was both a means of personal expression and a bond that united them.

Clara Wieck was born on September 13, 1819, in Leipzig, Germany. From a very young age, she was considered a child prodigy on the piano, thanks to the rigorous musical education provided by her father, Friedrich Wieck, a renowned music teacher. By the age of nine, Clara was already giving concerts in Europe, being acclaimed for her technical virtuosity and her interpretative ability.

Clara was not only an outstanding pianist, but also a composer, something unusual for women of her time. However, despite her achievements, her role as a woman in 19th-century society constantly placed her in the shadow of men, including her future husband, Robert Schumann. This situation created tensions throughout her life, as Clara had to balance her musical career with her role as a wife and mother of eight children.

Robert Schumann was born on June 8, 1810, in Zwickau, Germany. From a young age, he showed a great interest in music and literature, which deeply influenced his creative approach. He began studying piano with Friedrich Wieck, Clara's father, but an accident to his right hand kept him from his dream of becoming a virtuoso pianist. Instead, he devoted himself to composition and, later, to music criticism, founding an influential magazine, Neue Zeitschrift für Musik.

Robert is considered one of the greatest composers of the Romantic period. His music is imbued with deep lyricism and poetic approach. His works, especially the piano pieces, songs, and symphonies capture the emotional complexity of the human being, and many of his compositions were inspired by his love for Clara.

Clara and Robert met when she was just nine years old, and Robert was a piano student of her father. As Clara grew older, Robert began to fall in love with her, recognizing her musical talent and feeling a deep emotional connection. However, their romance was complicated from the start. Clara's father, Friedrich Wieck, fiercely opposed the relationship, as he feared that Robert would not be a good match for his daughter, due to his emotional instability and lack of financial stability.

Despite Friedrich's objections, Clara and Robert continued their relationship in secret. After a long legal and emotional battle with Clara's father, the couple finally married on September 12, 1840, just a day before Clara's 21st birthday. This event marked the beginning of one of the most iconic marriages in the musical world.

Clara and Robert's relationship was an inexhaustible source of mutual inspiration. Their love was deeply reflected in their music, with Robert composing many pieces dedicated to Clara, such as his "Liederkreis, Op. 39" and "Dichterliebe, Op. 48". Clara, for her part, was the main interpreter of Robert's works, helping him to establish himself as a composer.

Clara was not only Robert's muse but also his closest critic. Her skills as a pianist allowed her to offer him valuable advice on his compositions, and her emotional support was crucial during the bouts of depression and mental breakdown that Robert suffered throughout his life. Together, they formed an artistic couple that challenged the social conventions of their time, showing how love and creativity could fuel each other's work.

Despite having to care for a large family, Clara never stopped playing and composing music, being one of the few women of her time who managed to maintain an artistic career while raising children. In many ways, she was a pioneer, proving that marriage and motherhood were not incompatible with an artistic life.

Despite their deep love, Clara and Robert's relationship was not without its difficulties. The main challenge was Robert's mental health. Throughout his life, he suffered from mental disorders, which worsened over the years. In 1854, following a suicide attempt, Robert was committed to a psychiatric hospital, where he spent the last two years of his life. This was a devastating blow to Clara, who continued to work and raise her children while dealing with the grief of seeing her husband succumb to insanity.

Another negative aspect was the personal sacrifice Clara had to make for her marriage. Despite her incredible talent as a composer, Clara often put her ambitions on hold to support Robert's career. While she was one of the most acclaimed pianists of her time, her compositions did not receive the same recognition, partly due to the limitations imposed by patriarchal 19th-century society and the fact that Clara herself prioritized her husband's works.

The love story between Clara and Robert Schumann has endured over time, not only because of the emotional intensity of their relationship but also because of the impact they both left on the world of music. Their letters, in which they discussed both matters of daily life and their musical musings, reveal a deep connection based on love and mutual respect.

After Robert died in 1856, Clara dedicated the rest of her life to preserving his legacy. She continued to give concerts well into her old age and was responsible for the publication of many of Robert's works. However, her legacy was also cemented over time. Today, Clara is recognized not only as Robert Schumann's wife and muse but also as one of the greatest pianists in history and a composer who deserves her place in the pantheon of classical music.

16. Simón Bolívar and Manuela Sáenz: A story of love and revolution

The story of Simón Bolívar and Manuela Sáenz is wrapped up in the drama of the struggle for Latin American independence, uniting their lives not only by love but by the common ideal of freedom. This relationship between the Liberator and the Quito heroine has transcended time not only for its romantic dimension but also for its historical relevance in one of the most significant moments of the continent. The love of Bolívar and Sáenz stood out for its intensity, loyalty, and its key role in the political events of the time. However, it was also marked by the difficulties and contradictions of war and political circumstances.

Simón Bolívar (1783-1830) is one of the most iconic figures in Latin American history. Born in Caracas, Venezuela, he was a military and political leader who played a central role in the independence of several South American countries, including Venezuela, Colombia, Ecuador, Peru, and Bolivia. Educated in Europe, Bolívar was influenced by the ideals of the Enlightenment and by the ideas of liberty, equality, and popular sovereignty.

Known as El Libertador, Bolívar dedicated his life to liberating South America from Spanish rule. His vision of a united America free from the colonial yoke was the driving force of his life, although his dream of a unified Spanish America was never realized. Despite military and political successes, Bolívar lived through many moments of frustration and betrayal, which led him to renounce his public life in his later years, going into exile in Santa Marta, Colombia, where he died in 1830.

The other protagonist, Manuela Sáenz (1797-1856) was a woman ahead of her time. She was born in Quito, Ecuador, to a well-off family, but her life was marked by a strong independence of thought and action. From a young age, Manuela showed an inclination towards politics and the defense of women's rights, something uncommon in the conservative and patriarchal society of the time. Her marriage to an English merchant led her to live in Lima, where she began to actively involve herself in revolutionary politics.

Manuela was not only a passionate lover of Simón Bolívar but also a key figure in the fight for independence. She earned the nickname "The Liberator's Liberator" for her bravery and dedication to the revolutionary cause. In 1828, she was responsible for saving Bolívar's life when a group of conspirators tried to assassinate him in Bogotá, an event that cemented her place in history. In addition, she was recognized for her participation in several battles and her role as a political leader in the independence campaign.

Simón Bolívar and Manuela Sáenz met in 1822 in Quito, at a time when Bolívar was already a prominent figure in the fight for Latin American independence. The meeting between Bolívar and Manuela occurred amid celebrations for the liberation of Quito after the Battle of Pichincha. Manuela, fascinated by Bolívar's charisma and idealism, was deeply impressed. Bolívar, for his part, found in Manuela not only a romantic partner but a valuable political ally and a woman with a determination that matched his own.

Their relationship quickly consolidated, and Manuela joined Bolívar on his military campaigns, becoming his advisor and confidant. Despite the criticism she received for breaking with the conventions of the time, Manuela defied social norms to be with the man she loved and whom she supported in his revolutionary mission. From then on, their lives became intertwined, both by the love they shared and by the common cause that united them.

The romance between Simón Bolívar and Manuela Sáenz was not only a love story, but also an alliance of ideals. Manuela was not simply Bolívar's lover; She was an active collaborator in his fight for independence, accompanying him on campaigns, encouraging the troops, and providing invaluable emotional and strategic support. Her bravery, demonstrated in events such as the assassination attempt in Bogotá in 1828, made her a central figure in Bolívar's life.

They both shared a passion for Latin American independence and a desire to free oppressed peoples from colonial rule. Manuela was a loyal and devoted companion, willing to sacrifice her safety and reputation to stand by Bolívar and aid his cause. For Bolívar, Manuela was more than a sweetheart; she was an emotional pillar that sustained him in his moments of greatest discouragement and exhaustion, especially in the last years of his life, when political divisions and betrayals led him to lose faith in his dream of American unity.

However, the relationship between Bolívar and Manuela also had dark and complicated aspects.

Although they were deeply in love, their love could never be formalized in conventional terms. Bolívar, although separated from his wife María Teresa Rodríguez del Toro, to whom he was briefly married before being widowed, never married Manuela. The irregular nature of their love affair attracted criticism from both Bolívar's political enemies and the conservative society of the time.

Manuela also suffered the consequences of her love for Bolívar. Despite being a free-spirited woman, her association with the Liberator and her involvement in politics and military campaigns marginalized her socially. Following Bolívar's death in 1830, Manuela was exiled from Colombia and spent the rest of her life in poverty and oblivion in a small coastal town in Peru, where she died in 1856. The relationship, which during Bolívar's lifetime had been a bond of shared passion and struggle, was transformed after his death into a memory that relegated her to the margins.

The love story between Simón Bolívar and Manuela Sáenz has endured throughout the centuries, not only because of its passionate nature but because of the historical context that surrounded them. The relationship between the two symbolizes the union of two beings who loved each other deeply, but also the union of two revolutionaries committed to the freedom and independence of Latin America.

Manuela Sáenz has been vindicated in modern times as a feminist icon and a key historical figure who challenged the norms of her time. Her role as a fighter in the war of independence and her ability to act on equal terms with men at a time when women were relegated to secondary roles have made her a heroine, especially in the feminist and civil rights movements.

On the other hand, Bolívar and Manuela's love is also interpreted as a tragedy, given that their relationship was not only interrupted by political struggles, but also by social expectations that prevented their love from being fully accepted. Even so, the devotion of both has been immortalized in history as one of the great romances of the continent, a mix of passion, loyalty, and sacrifice for an ideal greater than themselves.

17. Elizabeth Taylor and Richard Burton: A romance of passion and torment

The relationship between Elizabeth Taylor and Richard Burton is one of the most intense and turbulent love stories in the history of cinema. Known as much for their dazzling talent as for their scandalous personal lives, their romance has endured in the collective memory for its intensity, its dramatic ups and downs, and their unwavering mutual attraction. Throughout their life together, Taylor and Burton experienced the most passionate side of love, as well as the challenges that come with a romance full of excess, conflict, and reconciliation. This story has transcended time as a symbol of the duality of love: the glory of emotional connection and the dangers of emotional chaos.

Elizabeth Taylor (1932-2011) was one of the most famous actresses of her time, known as much for her dazzling beauty as for her acting talent. She was born in London to American parents and began her career in film at an early age. During her career, she won two Academy Awards for Best Actress, establishing herself as one of Hollywood's biggest stars. Films such as Cleopatra (1963), and Who's Afraid of Virginia Woolf? (1966) and Cat on a Hot Tin Roof (1958) marked her career and showed her ability to play complex and emotional characters.

However, Taylor's private life was as fascinating as her film career. She was married a total of eight times, two of them to Richard Burton. Her relationship with him was undoubtedly the most famous and controversial of all, due to its intensity, its multiple breakups and reconciliations, and the media coverage they received.

In turn, Richard Burton (1925-1984), a Welsh actor with prodigious talent, was famous for his deep voice and his ability to play dramatic roles on stage and in film. Throughout his career, he was nominated seven times for an Academy Award, although he never won. Coming from humble beginnings in Wales, Burton worked hard to become one of the most respected actors of his generation, both on stage and in Hollywood.

However, like Taylor, Burton also lived a life of excess. Fame, wealth, and alcohol played a central role in his life, and these elements were both a blessing and a curse in his relationship with Elizabeth Taylor.

Elizabeth Taylor and Richard Burton met in 1962 on the set of Cleopatra, the epic film that told the story of the legendary Egyptian queen and would become one of the most expensive productions in history. Taylor, who played Cleopatra, and Burton, who played Mark Antony, became involved in a torrid romance during filming. At the time, they were both married to other people, causing a media scandal.

Their mutual attraction was undeniable and electrifying. Taylor described Burton as one of the most fascinating men she had ever met, while Burton was captivated by Taylor's beauty and strong character. The intensity of their relationship during the filming of Cleopatra was so evident that it even overshadowed the film's release itself, as the tabloids focused on the forbidden romance between the two stars.

The scandal soon hit the media, and their relationship became the subject of worldwide speculation and fascination. Both divorced their respective spouses and married in 1964, beginning one of Hollywood's most famous and complex marriages.

Over the years, Taylor and Burton shared a deep emotional connection, filled with love and mutual admiration. Their relationship was passionate, and they both proved to be a vibrant couple, both on and off screen. Together they starred in 11 films, the most memorable being Who's Afraid of Virginia Woolf? (1966), which earned them great critical praise for their heartbreaking and raw performances.

Personally, Taylor and Burton supported each other through difficult times. Richard Burton described Elizabeth as his "emotional anchor" on several occasions, and their love was an emotional refuge amid the frenzy of their public lives. Taylor, known for her loyalty to those she loved, also helped Burton confront his inner demons, especially about the alcoholism that marked Burton's life.

Despite the fights and ups and downs, the love between Taylor and Burton never completely disappeared. In his letters, Burton wrote about his unwavering love for Elizabeth, and she always considered him the love of her life, even after their second separation.

However, the relationship between Elizabeth Taylor and Richard Burton also had a dark side. Both led excessive lifestyles, full of alcohol, parties, and luxury, which aggravated personal and relationship problems. The arguments between them were as intense as their love, leading to multiple breakups.

Burton's alcoholism was a constant source of tension in their marriage. Arguments and erratic behavior caused by alcohol abuse wore down their relationship. Both were people with strong and temperamental personalities, which led to constant clashes. In 1974, after ten years of marriage, the couple divorced, although they remarried the following year, in 1975. Their second marriage lasted only a year, and they divorced for good in 1976.

Excess and fame also took a toll on their emotional well-being. Burton, despite his love for Taylor, struggled with feelings of inferiority, especially in comparison to Elizabeth's enormous popularity and magnetism. On the other hand, Taylor was often frustrated by Burton's inability to overcome his problems, which led to a toxic dynamic at times.

The love story between Elizabeth Taylor and Richard Burton remains one of the most famous and talked about in Hollywood. Their relationship symbolizes the intensity of passionate love, but also the dangers of obsession and excess. Both, as icons of cinema, left an impressive legacy in the history of the industry, but their romance is remembered as a combination of the greatness and chaos that love can bring.

Through their letters, books, and interviews, it has become clear that, despite the difficulties, the love they shared was genuine and deep. Burton once wrote about Taylor: "I loved you more passionately than any other woman was loved in the history of mankind." Taylor, for her part, always kept a special place for Burton in her heart, even after his multiple marriages and subsequent relationships.

18. Paul Gauguin and Teha'amana: Art, Colonialism and Controversy in Tahiti

The relationship between Paul Gauguin, the famous French post-impressionist painter, and Teha'amana, a young Tahitian woman, has sparked both fascination and controversy over time. This bond, which began in the context of European colonialism in the South Pacific, has been interpreted in various ways: as a romantic or exploitative relationship, as a source of artistic inspiration, or as an example of the power imbalances and colonial dynamics of the time. Its impact on Gauguin's work is undeniable, but the implications of their relationship have left a problematic legacy that is difficult to ignore.

Paul Gauguin (1848-1903) is one of the most influential names in the history of Western art. Born in Paris, Gauguin worked as a stockbroker before devoting himself fully to painting in the 1880s. Inspired by Impressionism, but seeking to break away from the artistic conventions of his time, Gauguin sought what he considered a "primitive" way of life, removed from the industrialized society of Europe. This search took him to the islands of the South Pacific, particularly Tahiti, in 1891.

In Tahiti, Gauguin hoped to find an exotic paradise that matched his idealized vision of a simpler life closer to nature. However, what he found was a culture already influenced by French colonization. Despite this, he decided to remain there, seeking inspiration for his art and, in his personal life, a connection to the local culture.

Soon after he arrived in Tahiti, Gauguin met Teha'amana, a young native girl who, according to records, was around 13 years old when she began her relationship with the painter, who was already in his 40s. The age difference and the colonial context have caused this relationship to be viewed in a critical light today. At the time, however, it was common for European colonizers to take native wives, a practice that reflected the power imbalances inherent in colonialism.

Teha'amana, whose life before meeting Gauguin is little known, became the artist's "vahiné" (wife) under local custom. This relationship inspired much of the art Gauguin produced during his stay in Tahiti. Teha'amana appears in several of his best-known paintings, such as Spirit of the Dead Watching (1892), which depicts a naked, seemingly vulnerable young woman in a position that many critics have interpreted as a combination of fascination and exoticization on Gauguin's part.

From an artistic perspective, the relationship between Gauguin and Teha'amana had a profound impact on the painter's work. The time he spent with her and his immersion in Tahitian culture provided the material and inspiration for some of his most iconic pieces. His depictions of Polynesian life, though idealized, broke with the conventions of Western art and contributed to the development of symbolism in painting.

The influence of Teha'amana and Tahitian culture on Gauguin also led him to experiment with the use of color and form in radical ways. His depictions of native life, though often criticized for being a mixture of fantasy and reality, opened a new era in Western art by challenging European canons of beauty and representation.

In addition, Gauguin drew inspiration from local spiritual beliefs and Tahitian myths to develop a series of paintings that explored themes such as death, and the meaning of existence – themes that became recurrent in his later work. Without Teha'amana and his life in Tahiti, Gauguin may not have reached the artistic heights for which he is remembered today.

However, the relationship between Gauguin and Teha'amana is also a reflection of the colonial tensions of the time and the problematic attitudes that Europeans, including artists, had towards colonized peoples. In retrospect, the bond between the two has been criticized for its marked imbalance of power. Teha'amana, like many other indigenous women at the time, was a victim of a colonial structure that allowed Europeans to exploit and dominate both natural resources and people.

Gauguin, who referred to Tahiti as a "primitive paradise," approached his relationship with Teha'amana from a paternalistic and exoticizing perspective. His paintings of her, while beautiful from a technical standpoint, are an example of the idealized "other" that Western artists often projected onto non-European cultures. Depictions of Teha'amana tend to strip her of her agency, presenting her as a passive figure subservient to the artist's desires and fantasies.

Another problematic aspect of their relationship was the fact that Gauguin, despite his relationship with Teha'amana, continued to lead a chaotic and self-destructive life. He is known to have contracted syphilis, a disease that he likely passed on to Teha'amana, as he did to other partners. His love affairs and riotous lifestyle took a toll on the health of those around him, and Teha'amana was no exception.

Furthermore, Gauguin never fully engaged with Tahitian life. Despite his fascination with the culture, he always maintained a critical distance and returned to Europe on several occasions, leaving Teha'amana and other aspects of his life in the Pacific behind. His relationship with Tahiti was, in many ways, superficial and marked by an unequal relationship between the colonizer and the colonized.

The legacy of the relationship between Paul Gauguin and Teha'amana remains a matter of debate and reflection. On an artistic level, paintings inspired by Teha'amana and his time in Tahiti remain some of Gauguin's best-known and most influential works. Works such as Manao Tupapau and Where Do We Come From? What Are We? Where Are We Going? has inspired generations of artists and critics to rethink notions of the "primitive" and the "exotic" in Western art.

However, modern criticism has highlighted the problematic power dynamics that defined the relationship between Gauguin and Teha'amana, and how these reflect colonial tensions and the exploitation of indigenous peoples by European colonizers. Gauguin has been criticized for romanticizing and exoticizing Tahitian culture while contributing, directly or indirectly, to the exploitation of the people who lived there.

Today, the relationship between Gauguin and Teha'amana is a reminder of how the art and personal lives of great artists cannot be separated from the historical and political contexts in which they developed. Although their romance has been an object of fascination, it is also a testament to the destructive effects of colonialism on the lives of the most vulnerable people.

19. Margaret Fuller and Giovanni Angelo Ossoli: A love between revolutions and tragedy

The life of Margaret Fuller (1810-1850), one of the most prominent intellectuals of the 19th century, and her relationship with Giovanni Angelo Ossoli (1801-1850), an Italian nobleman committed to the revolutions of his time, represents one of the most fascinating love stories of the Romantic period. Their romance was, in many ways, a symbol of the social, political, and cultural changes unfolding around them. The combination of their mutual commitment to revolutionary ideas, their passionate love, and the tragic conclusion of their life together has given this relationship lasting significance.

Sarah Margaret Fuller was a writer, journalist, literary critic, and feminist who was part of the transcendentalist movement in the United States, along with figures such as Ralph Waldo Emerson and Henry David Thoreau. Fuller was the first woman to be editor of the influential newspaper The Dial, one of the leading publications of transcendentalism, and she was also the first foreign correspondent for an American newspaper, working for the New York Tribune.

An advocate of women's rights and gender education, Fuller is remembered for her book Women of the Nineteenth Century (1845), one of the first feminist texts in history. In it, she argued for equal opportunities and independence for women, radical ideas for her time.

On the other hand, Giovanni Angelo Ossoli was an Italian count, a descendant of a noble family that had lost part of its power and fortune. Although at the beginning of his life, he was not deeply involved in politics, the political turmoil in Italy and his meeting with Margaret Fuller led him to embrace republican ideals and to commit himself to the revolutionary struggles of the nineteenth century.

Italy at that time was fragmented into several states under the influence of foreign powers, such as Austria, and was struggling for its unification. Ossoli joined the revolutionary movements that wanted a unified Italy free of foreign domination, actively participating in the Revolutions of 1848, which shook Europe and sought to end absolute monarchies and establish democratic republics.

Margaret Fuller arrived in Europe in 1846 as a correspondent for the New York Tribune, and her stay in Italy marked a radical change in her life. In 1847, she met Giovanni Angelo Ossoli in Rome, when she was already immersed in the city's hectic political environment. Although Fuller came from an intellectually vibrant background in America, her personal life had been marked by a rejection of conventions, especially in terms of marriage and romantic relationships. Ossoli, with his youth and revolutionary spirit, immediately attracted her.

The love between Fuller and Ossoli began amid revolutionary turmoil, and the relationship was not only a sentimental connection but also a political and emotional partnership. Despite their social and cultural differences, as Fuller was an intellectual with progressive ideas and Ossoli was an Italian aristocrat, their relationship prospered amidst the chaos of the European revolutions.

The couple had to keep their relationship secret for a time, as Ossoli came from a conservative aristocratic family that opposed his relationship with an American woman and because at that time marriage between people of different social classes was frowned upon. Despite this, they married secretly in 1848 and, shortly after, had a son, Angelo Ossoli, in 1849. This child was born in a context of uncertainty, both due to the political tensions that engulfed Italy and the nomadic and clandestine life that Margaret and Giovanni led.

During the revolutions of 1848–49, Fuller and Ossoli were active participants in the Roman Republic, a brief period in which Rome was proclaimed a republic, attempting to establish a democratic government at the center of papal power. Ossoli enlisted in the Roman National Guard and fought on the barricades, while Fuller worked as a nurse and wrote passionately about republican struggles for her American readers. This experience brought them together deeply and solidified their commitment to each other.

The relationship between Margaret Fuller and Giovanni Ossoli was a remarkable example of love based on shared ideals and mutual respect. Despite their cultural and class differences, their love blossomed amidst an unstable political context, showing the power of common commitment. Fuller, throughout her life, had rejected traditional models of marriage and gender relations and found in Ossoli a man who respected her intellectual independence and her role as a thinker. Furthermore, they both shared a passion for justice and freedom, values that united them deeply.

Their relationship was also an example of love that transcends borders, as Fuller, an American, and Ossoli, an Italian, forged a life together in the context of the European revolutions. Their love story symbolizes the fusion of cultures and the possibility of finding a deep connection despite external differences.

However, there were also significant difficulties in their relationship. The life they led was marked by uncertainty and danger, due to the revolutions in which they were involved. The couple faced economic challenges, as Ossoli had lost his fortune and Fuller had no stable financial means. In addition, their relationship was largely clandestine, adding to the tension and logistical difficulties, especially with a newborn son.

Tragically, the relationship was abruptly cut short. After the fall of the Roman Republic and the suppression of revolutionary movements, the couple decided to return to America in 1850 with their son. However, the ship they were traveling on, the Elizabeth, was wrecked off the coast of Fire Island, New York, and both Margaret, Giovanni and their son Angelo died. Fuller had brought with him his most recent manuscript, a work on the history of the Italian Revolution, but it was also lost at sea.

The love story between Margaret Fuller and Giovanni Angelo Ossoli has transcended for several reasons. First, it is one of the first modern stories of a woman who challenged the social, intellectual, and emotional conventions of her time. Fuller was not only a pioneer in the fight for women's rights but was also a key figure in literature and journalism. Her relationship with Ossoli was not only a matter of love but also a partnership based on shared ideals of justice and freedom.

Moreover, the tragic death of both in the shipwreck adds an element of romantic legend to their story, consolidating them as a couple whose aspirations and hopes were cut short by fate. The relationship between Margaret Fuller and Giovanni Ossoli is remembered not only for their love but also for the revolutionary context in which it arose, becoming a symbol of the social and political struggles of their time.

20. Ernest Hemingway and Hadley Richardson: Love, Betrayal and Nostalgia

The relationship between Ernest Hemingway and Hadley Richardson is one of the most captivating love stories in the life of the famous writer. Often remembered by Hemingway as the purest and most meaningful relationship he ever had, his marriage to Hadley, though brief, left an indelible mark on his personal life and literary career. Their romantic relationship, filled with love, sacrifice, and, ultimately, betrayal, has transcended time both for its influence on Hemingway's work and for the emotional complexity that surrounded it.

Ernest Hemingway met Hadley Richardson in 1920, when he was 21 and she was 28. Hadley, a shy and reserved woman, had grown up in St. Louis in a strict family and, until meeting Hemingway, led a quiet life. Hemingway, on the other hand, was an ambitious and charismatic young man who had just returned from World War I, where he had been wounded. His adventurous spirit and determination to become a writer made him seem older than he was. Despite their age difference, the two formed a quick and intense bond.

They married in 1921, and soon after, they moved to Paris, which at the time was the epicenter of the artistic and literary avant-garde. Paris provided the couple with a vibrant and stimulating environment, where Hemingway began to interact with key figures of the so-called "Lost Generation," such as F. Scott Fitzgerald, Gertrude Stein, and Ezra Pound. For Hadley, who was unfamiliar with the literary world, it was a radical change. However, she always supported Hemingway in his ambition to become a recognized writer.

During the years they spent in Paris, Hadley was Hemingway's emotional pillar. She supported the couple financially thanks to an inheritance, allowing Hemingway to concentrate exclusively on writing. This period in Paris was fundamental to Hemingway's development as a writer. His first successes, including the publication of his short stories and the writing of his first novel, The Sun Also Rises, came in these years of domestic stability provided by Hadley.

Although the relationship was marked by love and mutual support, the marriage was not without its difficulties. Hemingway's growing fame in literary circles exposed him to new temptations and pressures. His social life became more intense, and while Hadley tried to adapt to the bohemian life of Paris, he always seemed to be one step behind. Although he provided her with all possible emotional support, the difference between their personalities became increasingly apparent. Hemingway was dynamic and passionate, while Hadley was more introverted and conventional.

The beginning of the end came when Hemingway met Pauline Pfeiffer, an American fashion journalist who quickly became involved in the couple's life. Pauline, a sophisticated and ambitious woman, began an affair with Hemingway while he was still married to Hadley. This love triangle puts enormous pressure on the marriage. Although Hadley was deeply in love with Hemingway, she eventually discovered the infidelity, which led to an emotional crisis in the couple.

In 1926, Hadley decided to end her marriage to Hemingway. The divorce was finalized in January 1927, and shortly afterward, Hemingway married Pauline. The breakup of his relationship with Hadley was an emotional blow to Hemingway, who on several occasions expressed remorse for how things had ended. In his later writings, Hemingway often reflected on the pain of losing Hadley, going so far as to call her "the best part of my life."

Although their marriage only lasted six years, the relationship between Hemingway and Hadley left a profound impact on both. For Hadley, it was a life-changing experience that defined her adult life. Following the divorce, she returned to the United States, where she lived a quieter life, moving away from the literary spotlight. Hemingway, on the other hand, continued a tumultuous love life, marrying three more times, but never again finding the same peace and emotional stability that he had with Hadley.

Hemingway's love for Hadley was immortalized in his work. In his novel A Moveable Feast, a memoir about his years in Paris, Hemingway devoted several pages to his relationship with Hadley, describing her as the woman who supported him when no one else believed in him. It is in this book that Hemingway expressed his deep nostalgia for those early years in Paris and for the love he shared with Hadley, mourning the loss of what was once a happy and simple life. In one of the most poignant lines in the book, she wrote, "When we were very poor and happy."

The positive side of their relationship was Hadley's unconditional support during the early and most difficult years of Hemingway's career. Her love and sacrifice allowed Hemingway to flourish as a writer, giving him the time and space necessary to develop his art. In many ways, Hadley was the silent force behind Hemingway's early success.

On the other hand, the negative side of their relationship was Hemingway's eventual betrayal. Although he was a passionate and charismatic man, his inability to be faithful and his constant search for new experiences led him to break Hadley's trust. This pattern of behavior followed him throughout his life, repeating itself in his later marriages.

The relationship between Ernest Hemingway and Hadley Richardson reflects the ups and downs of love and marriage. Their story is a mix of romance, sacrifice, betrayal, and regret. For Hemingway, Hadley represented the stability and support he needed in the early years of his career, but his desire for adventure and new excitement led him to destroy what had been a deep love. Through his writing, Hemingway immortalized Hadley, showing us that although their relationship ended, the impact it had on his life lasted forever.

Other books by the author Phillips Tahuer that you will find on this platform:

• The greatest conspiracy theories
• Great robberies in history
• Famous murderers - the perverse side of the mind-
• Lives in captivity - Stories of real kidnappings-
• Agents, informants, and traitors - the world of espionage-
• Pirates of the 21st century
• Tragic loves
• 30 curiosities of World War II
• Dark experiments on humans
• Real-life heroes
• Powerful men in modern history
• Lessons in practical psychology